Black Snowman

BLACK SNOWMAN

BLACK SNOWMAN

Also by Olivia

Neverland

Black Snowman

Written & Illustrated by

OLIVIA REMSANGPUII

BLACK SNOWMAN

For Snow,

In another life,
I will find you
before anyone could hurt you.

CONTENTS

INTRODUCTION

Chapter I
The Writer

Chapter II
Black Snowman

ACKNOWLEDGEMENTS
ABOUT THE AUTHOR
A MESSAGE FROM THE AUTHOR

BLACK SNOWMAN

INTRODUCTION

"An angel born in hell."

This line, mentioned in this book in one of the poems, has been ruminating in my mind for a while now. The beauty and tragedy of finding someone who solely understands your soul, yet it is forbidden!

"If your dream includes someone besides you, you have no control over that dream!" said Aivi to Vernon. Maybe that's when I wanted to turn him into an art instead.

I claim no poetic power in these verses, for Black Snowman is a collection of poetry and prose about betrayal! The boy I met was as silent as the sea, and spoke no meaningful line! This book includes a chapter about the quiet man's untold narrative. If he had spoken, he ought to have said these lines to me.

I have always thought poems were keys to the heart, decoding the codes is the closest thing to holding the writer's heart— *thank you for holding mine.*

Black Snowman is a story dissected into poems with buried messages and hundreds of subtexts that delve into the fine line between two traitors who met when their hands were full yet decided to lend a helping hand to each other—*the tale of two traitors.*

I hope you decode the hidden messages and stories that must never be told inscribed in these poems and paragraphs! As a reader, imagine being in love with a character you read in a book, but you do not find that person in real life— in this book, the writer found him in real life but could not keep him, so she found a way to keep him, which is to cage him inside her art!

I hope you read Black Snowman from the perspective of the writer and snow! I hope you enjoy reading every single line written with guilt, regret & love, so much love.

With Guilt,

Olivia

Chapter I

The Writer

Once upon a time, there lived a writer who suffered with continuous sleep paralysis. She barely managed to put a smile on her face for years as everyone around her was slowly fading in her head. Her story did not inspire her to write a single poem for years until one cold winter, when she met a boy with the same illness who later became her muse.

As the writer quoted,

"My mind might fail me but my heart will always remember the soul that almost made her stop beating"

BLACK SNOWMAN

who are you?

a shivering summer

a frozen ice that melts easily

a snow so dark

i forgot it was ever white

no clue of who you are

no faintest idea of your family

the foggiest idea of your place

i can't pronounce it right

i do not know your past

but i feel like i could love you forever

if you tell me your name

—the day i met you

he craved the darkness
like the candle
that only feels seen
when the world forgets the sun

she craved the light
like the moth
still chasing
what was always meant to kill her

what is secret to one
is sacred to another
and though the blood may drip
not all of it is red

Two Traitors

Under the city of shame and blame,
there is a tunnel;
there is a place where traitors go,
a river they cross
chanting songs of regret;
o'er guilt stones and 'I was wrongs'.
Therefore in that place,
sold souls are not broken,
healers are not healed;
I shall meet you in that tunnel,
you who betrayed me before I did.

he held me like certainty

but still i ached

for the maybe in your eyes

and i kept polishing that glance

until it shone like a promise

that single glance

that could violate a poet

without a touch

the kind she still writes

on days when spring comes early

and all the flowers

look like

your goodbye

Hi Bye

I cross bridges with matches from witches

I bane foemen with poison from warlocks

I mourn mortals at cradles

—I say Hello and think Goodbye

unheld

we are the echo
of something older
than the body—
a song unplayed
on trembling strings

unheld
but never unloved

some loves
are not of this world
and this, my love—
this is one of them

some days

all i wish

is to overlook eternity

heaven and hell

karma and anything

in this entire universe

that stops me

from coming to you

heavens owe us

another less forbidden tale

one that does not demand mercy

forgiveness is

nodding it's fine

after being scarred

like the fragrance released

from a flower

after it's been crushed

not because it should

but because it must

f i v e

all these people
might never understand you
in this lifetime
and even in the next five
but i feel like I've listened
to the rhythm of your heart
and loved your silence
from our five previous lives

it does not matter to me at all
if you lie away
all my redundant future tensions
if it meant you'd stay
and when you told me
i was the only person
who made you feel understood

—that's when i knew i was important too

all these riches, beauty, power and fame

i put so high my entire life

couldn't make you mine, right?

we didn't hold each other's hands

and i will eternally be grateful to them

palms that did not get cut by his lies

and fingers that touched

only the strings of his guitar

cause the chief sinner in the room

must be the chief repenter in the room

and i was never ready

to repent for who could leave any dawn

and let go of these hands

but these hands

these brave hands

did not commit a sin

when the mind had committed

all the sins that could send me to hell

for a few drops

of your presence

i sat by the jars

i thought would be filled up

and by the door

stood my husband

waiting for me to go home

a lantern left burning

in an abandoned port

still flickers

at the sound of waves

though no ship

ever returns

to that shore

some things grow

just far enough

to ache

but never close enough

to bloom

NIGHT BEINGS

he stretched his arms widely

"You are my moon" said my heart

Give me the 4 o'clocks

blooming late night symphony

loyal lips and disloyal heart

—even though they both betrayed me

the smoke rings puffed through

o-shaped lips towards

the winking moon

you are my last sigh

a rhythm broken frontier

a nebulous dust trail

your celestial body

and my dark starry night

forever in collision

there is no way to have the moon

but we are night beings now

if his world ends in sorrows
i will take the fruit of pain
bite through all its deathbeds
swallow all his silent blues

and maybe
someday somewhere
he will read this page with a smile
thinking i was nothing
but happy

we shall meet again

where the black is so dark it looks bright

and the swan stops dancing when it rains

we shall meet there

where lying is not sin

and love is granted between three

we shall meet there

where confusion is love

and cigarettes speak secrets

—we shall never meet again

once upon a november
we dug two graves
the moon hung crooked that night
like a promise undone
and the stars refused
to witness what we became

a soul never mine
haunted every hallway of my heart—
like a hymn half-sung
in a language
i was never meant to know

something more sacred than love
and far more cruel

Dark Lies

as cold as you are
your smile kept me warm
tremble was my soul
when you scribbled my name
you walked with her
I wore his name
yours in Carnelian reds
mine in Sapphire blues
now that I no longer stay with you
I see you in places you've never been
you anointed a soul shaking sorrow
my battered and bruised soul lingered
but rich is the soul that loves the darkness,
sweet is the soul not slave to time
if a single piece of me was ever spared
I would've gladly crawled back to you
but with you
life is hell and death is heaven
I sensed it when my soul screamed
"Please poison me"

unfinished gods

i kissed your guilt

thinking it was love

i survived the clouds

believing them storms

may every kiss she gives

taste like what you lost—

and may the heavens

never forgive

the two of us

for mourning a future

we were never meant

to survive

there is an organ

inside of you

i desperately desired

and you'd be surprised

to know it's not your heart

—the brain that manipulates my heart

the quick-bending tree

will not last a month.

a season too intense

rarely survives the year.

valleys and farmlands

will never meet the sea.

—qui non sustinuit

there is a carillon bell above my room

please forgive me

for I have crossed the line

but when I close my eyes

we still meet in dreams

and I would gladly sleep away

for the rest of my life

but there is a carillon bell

above my room

and when it rings

my soul recalls all the sins

she has committed for you

years she spent thinking

she was the other woman

her voice shattered as she smirked

"I don't even see you in my dreams anymore"

for i have crossed the line

please forget me

she failed to unlove him
by loving others louder

gave his memory
to strangers—
wrapped in rhymes
he once inspired

she will always write his name
but he will never be the one
who survives the ending

Silent Vow

my last memories of him

exist beneath my fresh scars

i saw his footprints in the mud

and i went looking for him

i saw an empty lighthouse

that bear the same destiny as mine

i do not know if heavens will allow

two dark souls to collide again

but i do know

there is a destination

where we both agreed

to meet again

you lived

in every metaphor i buried

beneath softer names

your laugh—

a borrowed line

i gave to men

who never sounded like you

i will always write you

but you will never be

the one in those pages

only the sigh in between

that holds each word together

let it shiver

let it break

let it burn

let it cry

let it get haunted

or even run wild

—you are here to risk your heart

you hid from the same world

i ran toward barefoot

my name echoed through kingdoms

where they do not know yours

i spoke like i had a thousand lifetimes

while yours stayed sacred—

trying

was like braiding

silence with a song

fire with water

and light with darkness

two rivers

flowing toward different gods

two mountains

that would never move for each other

right where you left me

one day if you ever need me

you can always find me there

in between your hesitation and desire

sipping the wine you did not send me

talking about the tragedy

of biting down what can't be chewed

history speaks

on ears like yours—

to a regretful little boy

you will see my face

in battles between her lips,

knowing mine

would do no harm

and you will see me smiling

when you touch her soul

and grab her

like it was me

because my silence

will always be louder

than her screams

and her presence

will never

fill my absence

to surrender my heart to you,

even for a second,

is the most consequential

state of bewilderment,

and to imagine heading back

with a heart that's been rejected

a trillion times over

is the most absurd surmise,

but until the moment i perish,

surrendering my heart to you,

even for a blip in the radar,

is the easiest decision

this heart has ever

attempted to make.

you filled the hollows

i never spoke of

with laughter

that entered like it belonged

and kindness

that never kept count

you held my soul

like it was never hard to love—

like rain after a long drought,

like the arrival

of something starved so long,

it forgot its hunger

over and over again

those sinful eyes,

unforgiven grin,

tapered ribcage that formed

his V-shaped body;

skin as fair as mine,

hushed little lips

as quiet as the day i met him

—you are the only sin I would commit,

over and over again

always
heart to heart,
eye to eye—
but never
hand to hand
skin to skin

a hundred miles
between us
and a thousand sunrises
still won't
lead me to you

the map stayed folded
quiet on the table
i never learned
the language it spoke
but if maps could tear
beneath the weight of a look
ours would've crumbled
into a million pieces

he vowed

to freeze the clock

and kill all the milliseconds

that divided them

but little did he know

how she shattered her hourglass

and watched her remaining time

turn into nothing

in the waiting of

the *"still not fulfilled"* promises

—actions run faster than mere promises

you loved me

like i was your first miracle—

the first breath taken

after drowning

you spoke of forever

with hands that trembled,

like the sun had never risen

until i walked in

but all along

there was a man

whom i loved

like he was my first miracle—

the first breath taken

after drowning

i spoke of forever

with hands that trembled,

like the sun had never risen

until he walked in

—*first to you, second to me*

darkly fated

and they were unaware
that their souls would dance together
and the string would entangle
forming a promise in the stars
where it was destined forever

there is a legacy of legends

who once fought for their lovers

yet here we stand in denial

the ache I folded

into metaphors

the pause between sentences

you never carved

you lied i lined

words and boundaries

papers and wars

sonnets and combats

blues and scars

a living battle so undone

i am a sad poet with happy lines

and you are scared

i still seek your smile

in faces of passing souls

and my eyes

never to see you again

refuse to close

since the day you're gone

was never yours

is not yours

will never be yours

that's how the boy in black

with winter eyes

will always end up

in these verses—

o, my blackest snow,

my bluest sonnets,

scars I carved

into my own skin

Forbidden Desire

your somber eyes and silent glances

I lost it all, I lost it all darling

a grin can mask a tortured soul like mine

your soulless gaze, my microtonal cry

just how low did you think I'd go

to be your eleventh-hour

I'll find you even when they drug me

I'll hold your non-evidential existence

I'll find you where your paddy field

meets the garden in my mansion

I left your silence, you left my cacophony

I'll be gone and you may meet multitudes

beauties who could never be me

the atmosphere was heavy without you

now I refrain inhaling

you end me, I end you

and for some reasons

in the end there is no

'younme'

there is an abyss between our statuses

just like the crevasse

your existence is muted

no sound of breathing

no quantification of the span between us

but I know you are further forever than that

the winter's last gasp

amanitas nod their heads

to narcissus bloom

you are a perpetual covet

the bird I want to cage

my eternal desire

—you can love the whole world,

but next life

y o u   a r e   m i n e

some greeds are not greedy enough

the heavens never pried their hands

from what they desired most

some hungers do not anger the gods

they are left with treasures

but i

i must have wanted too wildly

and without a whisper

the heavens

dragged him away

no snow at sight in Tapesia

i only saw you, snow

a shivering winter it was

one night in November

it's the seventeenth day

white shirt black coat

red hair so so curly

a hundred miles away

from each other

when your fingers

slid through the strings

that's when all your melodies

entered my lonely life

and sometimes

darkness is the only thing

we know how to crawl into

when there is nothing else left to feel

but for you

it was always your home

and a light so bright

that humbles even the stars

may hang in the darkest skies

but will never dim her light

for you

prison is your glance, not a place

love is a feeling, not a gaze

when you said I felt like home

I knew you'd never find

your way back home

my love for him

was always louder

than the drums of his village

always gentler

than the hornbill

circling his land

but love to him

was only black and white

and love to me

will always be

all the colors

my eyes can see

i sometimes fear

that the weight of love

i carry for you

may shatter me one day

but you broke my heart

that night in February

and i let you

—you who made me ask for poison

he was my reflection
appearing only when
i looked in the mirror
always embraceable
never holdable

how could we end up together
if we are exactly the same soul
in different bodies

what if we agreed in a past life

to make it right in the next one

but here we are

breaking our vow.

—c'est celui-là

a black snowman

born of a winter without stars

bones sculpted from shadow

a smile carved in ice

a red sun

crowned in the glory of summer

warmth spilling gold

across the edges of the world

yet each time they drew near

snow wept into rivers at their feet

and still i came

again and again

to love what could not survive me

northern winds

carry hearts lost in winter's silence

miss songbird lost her voice

when you taught her silence

well if one time is enough

could it be forgiven?

or will it be forbidden?

did we ever end?

or even start?

please tell me that

every bridges between us didn't burn

cause i would've died for you

the night you melted

when i cried in Florence's arms

if seasons could stay still

and intentions could be seen

like leaves frozen mid-fall

you would have chosen me

right?

it took you five million seconds

to send me five little words

i wonder how long it will take

if one day you tell me to *wait*

—*i'll wait for forever*

heart iced in silence

soul shrouded in smoke

a quiet war within

where fire and frost

barely touch

we're a paradox

breathing life into cold

holding heat in shadows

there is an

invisible giant hole

in my heart

the ghosts of people

i cannot remember

are haunting me

forbidden love ends

with fate worse than collapse

they dare not crucify me

but you, darling

they will burn you to ashes

like witches once in love with magic

i claimed a piece of her

and put a piece of me

as i sat in her seat

i choked the wine she left

when i tried sipping as mine

it makes me memorable

usurpation of love

but it also makes me

no better than a thief

any color that touches black

will eventually turn black

i fought to keep my light

to not be swallowed whole

by a darkness that pulls and never lets go

that's the same struggle

we all carry inside

to hold our brightness

without losing ourselves to the dark

even when it feels as warm

as a black furry jacket

on a chilly winter night

one day I will leave you

forget that I used to love you

with the passion of a thousand men

you'd be the moon

left alone in the sky

the stars cannot solace him

when his Sun's forever gone

how does it feel to be abandoned

by the hands you would have died for

to watch them carry their warmth elsewhere

while you stand

with your winter

forever in your arms

and the memory of summer

burning holes through your chest

I would've died for him if he asked me to

but he was silent, as silent as *the tree*

that makes sound only when the wind visits

I spent my days sending poetic breeze

in that stillness

we both knew

if i go to him as i am

he won't survive

—the storm that fell for the tree

loving the poem

more than the muse

makes the poet

a merciless creature

even gods forbid

her from loving again

The Garden Of Agony

there is a garden of agony

where dark souls would sit together

in a *long-long swing*

humming their last lullaby

in that garden

you could hear a sad lullaby

he used to play

believe me

I thought I heard him

and I went looking for him

Love Never Fails

love is patient love is kind

love does not envy love does not brag love is not proud

love doesn't dishonor others

love doesn't seek its own way love is not easily angered

love takes no account of evil

love doesn't rejoice in unrighteousness

love rejoices with the truth

love bears all things

love believes all things love hopes all things

love endures all things

says 1 Corinthians 13

there's not a single line

we didn't follow

and yet with you

it was forbidden

there was happiness

but there was guilt

it was love

but it was sin

and when i failed

to take you with me

verse 8 confirmed

it was not love

—*love never fails*

it is true that i could never

look at you in the eye

not because those eyes hold fire

—fire cannot burn a dragon

but because I saw a sign of weakness

that mere fire could never show me

when your eyes met mine

—I saw a knife, to my future scars

Hope

I hope you think of me,

                —as I think of you.

I hope you listen to those blues,

                —and hear my voice.

I hope it burns your soul,

                —knowing I burnt mine for you.

I hope you see me every time you close your eyes,

                —the nightmare you can't escape.

my only love, you fade away
the scars remain, they stay the same
chased three hearts, one stopped beating
love lives on, in an empty shell
lies i know, which they don't
are eating you alive
and you will never know
the value of a woman
as long as little girls
make you smile

to play in the darkness and long for the light,

to play in the daylight and long for the dark.

—I don't know who you are

i was not lied to

i was not fooled either

the poison held a scent i knew

i drank it to the last drop

watched it bleed across my hands

and oh

how i welcomed

that liar

sleeps

in my avenue of frozen dreams

his waterlogged eyes glanced at mine

delivering a fleeting grin

his dad never spoke much

but praised my accent

he did not get hurt before we met

nor sleep with sad lullabies

he found me at fourteen

rescued my homeless soul

and sing me to sleep

it was a nice dream while it lasted

—but i can't sleep forever

the night insects sing outside my window

the same way they did when you were near

i write by the yellow bulb

the paper curling from the heat

somewhere in the hills a dog barks

and the echo feels like your name

i wonder if your nights sound like mine

or if kohima sleeps differently

my hand cramps before the page is full

but i keep writing to you in the dark

because silence is the cruelest sound

and letters are my only rebellion

I plucked a flower the other day, before it could even blossom.
In that very moment, I knew that flower was meant to be mine.
—*blooming or not*

the roof leaked during the monsoon

and the table was soaked by morning

a pile of my letters sat there

edges curling like dying petals

the ink bled into the paper

your name spreading into a blur

i thought of throwing them away

but i couldn't

they were the only proof

that i had spoken to you in my own language

even if the rain was the only one who listened

and the boy i write to will never understand them

The Author

the happy author who writes about sad endings

or the sad author who writes about happy endings;

who am I? Even I do not know!

but I do know,

even in the depth of my bluest days

I will always write you a happy ending.

fifty years from now

i may be the author

of a *hundred* books

with *thousands* of readers

but i will never end up

with the *one* i write to

unconditional treason

our quiet treason

between the part where our lies healed us

and the part where our honesty scarred us

there was happiness

no argument

no jealousy

no commitment

only happiness

you and me

H

A

P

P

Y

you faded like words

like promises and curses

i could not keep

no light

just the black little lamb

who barely fit in.

there are no more what-ifs

no sharp inhale at your name

just a soft, distant recognition

of a soul i once desired

i hope the songs we shared

do not sting when they play

i hope you find someone

who makes you feel superior

i hope she's younger and dumber

more obedient and less confident

—all the things i could never be

i do not wish for you to send me a song

i do not wish for you to call

i do not wish you back either

but i will always wish you

w e l l

My Favorite Fruit

As a kid, strawberry was my favorite fruit in the house and my most preferred ice-cream flavor.

As an adolescent, banana became my favorite ingredient for baking desserts.

I still remember lying on a sickbed as a small girl, craving sour mangoes, and feeling better after having a bowl.

As a teenage girl, it was most convenient to grab a fresh apple and take a bite.

Now, being in my early twenties, grapes and watermelon have become my favorite juice flavors.

But all this time, little did I know, it was the half cut lemon; half eaten & half abandoned in the corner of the fridge door that has stayed through all seasons of my life.

—this story is not about fruits

Therefore, it is hard to be a lemon in someone's life: half appreciated but treated like a pariah on the other side.

Lemons are sour, and over time they become bitter. Even a person who stays true to you can grow bitter one day and stop being there.

Lemons get sour and bitter,

a person has ups & downs.

My question to the person reading this is

—*Who is the lemon of your life?*

Is it your mom?

Is it the boy who said he'd wait for you?

Is it your dad who provides in silence?

Is it your sibling who unknowingly stays

when nobody else does?

or your grandma who secretly

gives away her own allowance?

Is it the shop owner you spend everyday with?

Now I want you to tell that person,

"You are the lemon of my life"

dead lover

winter sun

the cemetery

and mourning snow

he tossed me a glass

that was half full

a heart marred with

the scars of a dead lover

snow falls heavily

northern madness

frozen by our november fantasies

our december house

blue ballads and crimson souls

chasing her shadow

all his remaining life

hunting for the what-ifs

he drew a fine line between

the possibility of me

and his memories of her

—I could stand against

any soul draining spirit that surrounds you,

but I cannot compete with the dead.

we began with lies

heavens forbid

to end us with truth

her screams will never replace
my last whisper

you shall roam this world
searching for me
in passing souls
who will never
come close to the woman
you once deeply desired

and until the day you die
you will love no one but me

—curses

and on the judgement day

we would stand together

hold each other's hands

reminisce our tale

when God declared us innocent

for we have not committed

what heavens forbid

and deep down we both know

The Creator of all things

saw us that night

when we let each other go

with the tears of a thousand traitors

he once punished

not every muse

gets a monument

some are kept

like blood in the mouth

like ink that will never be spilled.

the sentence, left mid-breath—

some stories aren't written

because they hurt too beautifully

to end

the best things are never forced
they may take some time
lost their direction
or arrive bloodied
but never forced
never

he'll love you forever.

not the way a boy loves a girl

but the way a man loves his only defeat

he'll move on. he'll live. he may even marry.

but when he's lying next to someone else

on some quiet night

years from now—

he'll remember you

still *untouched.*

still *radiant.*

still *his greatest almost.*

let him keep that ache

and when he lay next to her

in those cold dark places

and imagine your face

he will die a hundred more times

said the voices, so i closed my eyes

and stopped looking for him

i stopped every idea of our almosts

November Nights

how badly did i desire your heart
the catalyst that alchemized me
lies i believed because you spoke them
my pen bled when you stopped waiting for me
but please remember

how i almost made you love me

Between Our Words

he spoke in log drums

and warrior chants

i spoke in choir songs

and harvest hymns

we could not trade our tongues

so we traded stories

over smoked pork and zawlaidi

you are a silent art piece

i must tear down

pain drained from plutocracy

words stolen from liars

you are a lying muse

gone are the days

when your lips

softly spoke my name

burnt are the eyes

i once dared to embrace

the life that is no longer mine

and the shell that still glitters

are all that remain in me

and the voices

you once admired so much

are now gone with the winds

you are the ghost haunting me,

but

you

are

not

even

dead.

beneath the towering ridges

the mist folds our words into quiet sighs

a fragile thread stretched over rugged lands

where stories cross but rarely stay

Aizawl breathes in morning prayers

Kohima hums with warrior echoes

two souls dancing in parallel shadows

separated by valleys, yet bound by time

the winding roads are rivers of memory

carrying hopes, fears, and forgotten songs

and though the distance is measured in miles

it is measured deeper in the spaces we leave behind

and even though we know

we won't catch one

some of us keep on chasing

the butterfly

only because it makes us happy

—*you who made me happy*

forever is the most brutal lie

but believe me when i say

you no longer cross my mind

when i see liars

and hear their vows

you will rather stay immortal

here inside my darkest art

in paragraphs of torture

and sonnets she will never read

such a pitiful soul

in the body of an angel

who knows nothing about

the dirty little secrets

between devils like

you and me

—blame me when she finds out

we tortured two souls

who did nothing

but loved us

we watered the garden

in which no flower grew

just because there was an old swing

i do not forget

how my *Lord* cast you

away from me

that night in June

in our peak of peace

dawn of happiness

and depth of love

but i do know that

He who sees my dying soul

will send you back to me someday

when i stop mourning

over a snow that has melted

on the hot summer night in June

i am a shipwreck

still in love

with the ocean

—just let me go

and *thirty years* from now

if one day somebody knocks on your door

and tell you there is a lady in *blonde*

waiting for you by the gate

i hope you go and get her

and never let me go again

when will this suffering end?

whenever I decide

where is the light?

wherever I decide

at the end of the day

night comes

at the end of the night

day comes

just because we need the rain,

does not mean

it should rain forever

the sun has to set,

humans must die

and you must leave

for we are mortals

for a reason

we shall not question

In valleys where the rivers part,

he walks in quiet, stoic grace;

a village boy in Kohima,

with guarded heart

and silence that holds a thousand faces.

she writes beneath the Aizawl sky,

her words like lanterns in the night;

a city girl with golden hands,

who pens the world in black and white.

their tongues divide like distant streams,

yet in the hush, their spirits blend;

not meant to cross in worldly schemes,

but bound in love that knows no end.

though fate may cast its heavy net,

and voices fail to weave their thread,

in silent gaze and heart's behest,

their souls converse, though words have fled.

and for the next few lifetimes

i will carry you with me

even in your stillness

i will listen only to your heartbeat

and no soul will dare to question

why i carry another heart beside my own

when there is a heart beating next to mine

—betrayal

do not worry about the secrets

you whispered away

in the wind

no one will remember

the darkest sins we committed

together in broad daylight

now i will sleep forever

under the carillon bell

that rings to torture my soul

whenever it calls your name

you'll be my muse

for centuries to come

and from this day

till my eternal rest

they will title me

as the writer who turned

the whisper of a silent man

into the echoes of heavens

all these people fell in love

with the idea of the life

they wished to have

but you fell in love with me—

and this heart will forever cherish

the knife that fell in love with an organ

and left her with no scar

everything around me is constantly dying

and i can hear my footsteps trembling

i cannot feel my heartbeat

no sign of an artist

no sound of *The Songbird*

now even the ghosts

are tired of listening to me

—*where are you?*

in a different timeline

i'd hug you a little longer

than that day

that dreary day in June

i'd cook you a fish

and you'd take me to see

the wrestlers in your area

i'd play the wooden guitar

from your father's backyard

and you'd sing for me

—all in a lifetime I'll never know

Threads of old promise tighten around him,

Echoes of ancestors whisper in the dark,

Tales told in morung fires, binding his fate,

Silence blooms where his heart dares not speak,

Every step mapped by rivers and hills he knows,

Open skies call to a path he cannot name.

The Sinner's Prayer

For I have envied my sister

I ask for Your forgiveness

For I have condemned a great sin

I ask for the Lord's mercy

For I have stolen somebody's happiness

and kept it as mine

Please have mercy on me

Forgive the pair of eyes

that kept an eye

on what's not hers

the molten core of your heart

still beats for the girl

who no longer recalls your name

and walks past you with a normal heartbeat

—you deserve to be forgotten

you desired my soul

i desired your heart

and till this day i wonder

how we landed on different ground

and we both lost our battles

—maybe our destinations were different

you left and i was willing to wait

for eternity and beyond

the skies witnessed our tragic ending

between falling star and fading scars

you left me with so much love

yet i deserve someone who is willing to stay

Voices drift across the divide,

Echoes tangled in unspoken tides,

Syllables slip through fingers like rain,

Ancient walls built by silent pain.

Yet beneath the fractured sound,

In silence, your pulse speaks to mine.

now that the light embraces me

i no longer dream of you

warm beams vow to serve me

no thoughts of you

now i carry us around

in sheets of the book

i will never explain

i inked your name

in dark sonnets

but you are somewhere

in the valley of Tapesia

wandering around

fighting for a love

that is not ours

we speak in glances

in pauses heavy as mountains

words trapped behind closed lips

tongues tied by customs and distance

between us lie rivers unnamed

valleys of meaning lost in translation

and every unspoken word

is a wound that never heals

i speak in stories no one hears

you listen in a language lost to time

and in this vast expanse of unspoken pain

we are strangers who once shared a heart

two worlds divided by ridges

two hearts separated by time

Kohima breathes in warrior songs

Aizawl hums with morning prayers

and though the sun warms both their lands

the space between remains unbridged

and in this quiet divide

they walk alone side by side

and since the day he's *gone*

this body has been dead

drowning in agony

and all the other sufferings that are left

but if tomorrow i wake up

and forget his name,

please thank the master

for the great deed

he's done for me

i might've loved him right

if i came from misted hills and smoky fires

where rivers roar with ancient drums

and silence lingers like carved stone

but i carry dawn's gentle prayers

soft winds that whisper through green valleys

and though our hearts beat close

we belong to separate worlds

they are sewing me back

into the person i was

before i met him

thread by thread

pill upon pill

until one day

i can walk past him

with a normal heartbeat

the curtain of our tale

has fallen before us

i have made peace

with watching you

from the shore

while you sail toward

a name

that is not mine

but if she ever holds you—

and picks up a pen

with the other hand

do not let her write you

do not let her turn your laugh

into metaphors

do not let her find the ache

i left behind

for there will always be

a part of me that believes

had we ever made it in this life,

would i have penned a gentler ending

the kind where love

survives the page

a happy ending kind of love

so in this one

—just do not let her write you

and for the last time

we hugged each other

as we bid our final goodbye

the skies did not

come down that day

to hold our cries

just two hearts saying goodbye

maybe i did not love you

as much as i love God

maybe loving you was

too big of a sin

i did not choose you for life

but you were never abandoned

for the sake of art

you may gaze upon your muse

with tender fire and longing

even bare, unguarded

without the weight of blame

without the stain of betrayal

—g

and one day

when you recall her face

do not look at the smile

a trap as warm as a fallacy's guile

look at her eyes

those solemn *"please save me"* eyes

the weight you carry

is flesh and bone

measured by years and sweat

will always be lighter

than the whisper of my first name

a silent legacy heavier than stone

it took me dying

for you to love me

it cost me death

to meet your soul

right from the beginning

my soul was not meant

for where you were going

someone had written a name on the wall

letters in white chalk

the rain would take them soon

but for now they clung to the brick

i traced the letters with my eyes

and thought of writing yours beside them

but i knew the rain would come

and wash us both away

still i held the thought

as if it could keep you here

for just a little longer

in a city that never truly saw me

you are still as beautiful as *the day i met you*

two nice people who were not nice to each other

two dark souls who lightened each other's path

now we are divided a thousand light years apart

and you are still as cold as *the day i left you*

in my dream we sat on the same bench

our knees almost touching

you told me about your father

and the river he loved

i told you about my mother

and her fear of bridges

we laughed softly

as if we had known each other for years

then the dream shifted

and i was on the bridge alone

the river below

too far to swim

and there

half-submerged in the current

was your father, reaching up to pull you in

while my mother stood at the far end of the bridge

calling my name, telling me not to cross

I'd be the star shining brightly in the sky;
you'd be down there
wishing on a star
that would never fall
for you again.

—healing

he never saw our future when he looked at my past

but when I saw how much he was burning

to keep me warm in that snowy winter day

for a fraction of a second

I forgot that hell exists

i knew you were not among my stars

yet i accepted you like a handmade curse

i once saw death in the smile

of a *blonde ruler*

when i looked in the mirror

and the emptiness in the eyes

of the person who once

was my everything

you did not see our future

when you looked at my past

i saw 'forever' struggling

to bind two effortless souls

who *believed* they were in love

you are a muse

my lying muse

and a tool

cannot be proud

just because the artist

held it once

with so much love

—stay silent forever

here I will stand

in correspondence with you

all these people love

each other with conditions

with commitment and passion

in a human way

but here I will stand

in correspondence with you

I will love you unconditionally

no expectation, no jealousy

you shall wander down the valley of life

meet lovers and taste their sweetness

touch the last poll, turn around

and return home to me

still, here I will stand

in correspondence with you

Dearest Snow,

I have carried your name
like a folded letter in my coat pocket
creased, worn,
but never opened in the daylight.

The world was never kind
to the way we met,
to the way my hands reached for yours
in shadows instead of streets.

History has always been cruel
to women like me
and to the men who would keep them.

Let's meet again in another lifetime
where they do not burn witches.
In that life,
I will live as I am,
and I will love you as I would have.

Never Yours,
Red

i did not tell you when they died

my love for you

has it been a week

or a lifetime ago?

you will never know

but i can feel you suffer

when you heard my whisper

in a room where i used to scream

i took a picture of the sunset

from the guesthouse balcony

the sky turning wild with reds and golds

i kept it in my phone

thinking i'd send it to you

but you left before i could

and now it feels wrong

to give you beauty

when you gave me

only half your presence

my heart's everlasting hope for us

has been broken down

by time's never ending attempt

to tear us apart

and even though our forever ends here

until the day i die

you will be loved

your bag was heavier than mine

but you carried it like a secret

i watched you walk ahead

your back a wall i couldn't climb

the train hissed

i wanted to run after you

but the platform swallowed me whole

and i became another passenger

with no ticket to your life

how tragic must your life be

to have melted completely in love with a soul

gone on to pen an entire book about him

and abandoned him

like all the other memories

—*wherever you are in this anarchic world,*

silently sitting in the corner,

waiting for me to love you again,

stay there,

I AM COMING.

BLACK SNOWMAN

Chapter II

Black Snowman

There lived a *snowman* in a small, frizzy Naga village who listened to a sad lullaby every day and never opened up—until he met *The Writer*, who changed him forever. He spoke so little, and silence was his language. If he had been able to write like *The Writer*, these are the poems and lines he would have written to her. This section of the book is the perspective of the *snowman*—the silent man's side of the story—observed and written by *The Writer* from his soulless gaze, silent smile, and meaningless words.

As you read his side of the story, I want you to read with understanding and love, just as *The Writer* once loved him—*with no blame and no doubt.*

—these are the words you'd have spoken to me right?

BLACK SNOWMAN

she was like a smoke

after the first puff

of an expensive cigarette

for a homeless heart like me

her soul was too expensive

to touch with bare hands

you stood where the hills met the fog

and called me by a name not mine

i answered anyway

our hands touched only in passing

like thieves

you spoke of the love of your life

as if he were a distant shore

and i, the storm

we swore our skies

would never meet

yet every night

you found my shadow

and fought all my wars

like you always knew

i was the loss of your life

our story didn't go down in history

but it echoed in every universe

that lies between us

stories that must never be told

and liars inside those lines

who must never be forgiven

once fell

madly in love

with so much guilt

she embraced my roots

way more than my flowers

she swallowed my flaws

like it was not hard

burned her own soul

in the process of feeding

my soul in hunger

and for that i will put her

above all souls

that will love my flowers

but never my roots

you are the prayer

i forget to say before bed

i never intended to leave a scar

on the girl who loved me sharp

you walked between lava and snow

and managed to smile

you are the anchor

to where this journey makes sense

i'm stuck here

with a love i no longer cherish

in a tangled circumstance

and there you are

entangled with an invisible cord

you will no longer cherish

when you get older

the moon might be hiding

but it is still there

i might never come close to you

but i will stay here forever

—forever in your shadow

your mother stitched red thread

into your wedding shawl

i swore i saw my breath in it

you told me not to

but i imagined tearing it apart

the drums beat in my village that night

i walked past the fire alone

clutching the beads you gave me

their heat burned through my palm

the smoke carried your scent uphill

to the house where you were kept

door barred

and groom inside

Salt on the Wind

my clan's feast smoke

drifted down to your side of the valley

I tasted salt in the wind

and knew you were laughing without me

I walked to the edge of the cliff

and you were there already

we spoke of the sea we had never seen

I told you I'd meet you there

you said it was too far to walk

but your eyes

had already made the journey

she knew my words

before i even spoke them

i do not need anyone

to give me butterflies

i need her

to calm my world again

the sky leans low tonight

over Tapesia's green terraces

as if it whispers my name

to the river she walks beside

the wind bends the bamboo

bowing to the ghosts of our hills

and somewhere between shadow and mist

i gather the pieces of a love

carried on footsteps that never meet

hidden where only valleys remember

I hope you understand

when my love is so silent

and words spoken are meaningless

and I hope you hear

the sorrow in my voice

when I say *"I see you"*

The First Crossing

she laughed like summer

yet stood with the poise of winter—

worshipped like a goddess

when i met her in august

everyone knew her name

and the name beside hers

spoken in one breath, *like prayer*

but that day

somewhere between fates and curses

her gaze crossed mine—

and this village boy forgot

who he was

forever

i crave your dark soul

in broad daylight

i long for someone

who has someone

and i do not mind

if our souls collide again

for the eleventh time

but it is such a sin

to raise hell

with somebody's happiness

and call it my salvation

mapless

we burned the map the night we met

so we could not find our way back

to what we were before

there is no home now

only the sea

and the small boat we keep rowing in circles

sometimes i think

we are not rowing anywhere

just writing the same letter over and over

hoping one day it reaches the other shore

you are the end of a sad lullaby

which promises to repeat itself

—*make me sleep*

i thought i would worship

the same God

my entire life

little did i know

a goddess would favor

this dying soul

and heal his scars

to you

i was just another clueless soul

to me

you were the light at the end of the tunnel

and for the first time

my soul longs for the light

—stay just for the night

fifty years from now

she will be an author

of a *hundred* books

with *thousands* of readers

but i will never end up

with the *only* woman

i've ever loved

even though they are meant

to never see you again

these eyes still look for you

in places you once reigned

and even though they will never hear again

these ears still fall for your voice

that lingers inside my head

Aizawl In Dreams

i've never walked her streets

but i have memorized them from her stories

the tea stalls at dawn

the hills rolling like a secret kept by clouds

the basketball court where they first fell in love

i will never stand there

not as her man

not as anything but a shadow

yet when i sleep

the city is mine

and she is waiting at every corner

you know the tragic part about losing a lover?

dead and long gone

you never said your *last goodbye*

you did not even break up

with that sweet soul

—i didn't even say goodbye

BLACK SNOWMAN

you danced with my soul

and left the body at the altar

you heard me before I even spoke

no division no quarter

my soul an eternal debt

to the girl who once bet

when nobody stayed true

to the boy listening blues

her brain outshines her beauty.

BLACK SNOWMAN

she ruled with a smile

but i have seen

the shadow in her laughter

she could make the river

change its course

and i let it carry me away

the man she loves the most

parades her like a trophy in daylight

but when the quiet hours come

and hearts cry to gods

she lets her heart fly into mine

like a scar the skin remembers

and i would take that bruise

again and again

BLACK SNOWMAN

what was it like to meet her? asked Love

it was like being caged in an island

being chased in heaven

a poison so sweet

a cave so bright

prison was her glance

not a place

the Sun in the summer sky

and I have to melt down

and risk my existence

to meet her

—*love story between the sun and a snowman*

BLACK SNOWMAN

he calls her by name

but i know the sound she makes

when her soul breaks

she gave him the world

and me her ruin

it is a cruel thing

to love someone this much

in silence

BLACK SNOWMAN

she died with my smile

or my smile died with her

i do not know

either way

they both died

BLACK SNOWMAN

i wished your love were gentler

a lantern not a wildfire

less a flood

more a river i could read

you drowned me in devotion

but never learned my tongues

every heart after yours

will glimpse your shadow in me

and curse you for it

BLACK SNOWMAN

i was not her favorite

she always placed me there

beneath her reputation

i always knew who i was

a first class insomniac

with eternal sleep paralysis

and damaged love life

i was not her favorite

i always knew what i was

and my hands will never

hold more than that

BLACK SNOWMAN

BLACK SNOWMAN

meet me where your chaos collide with my silence

where there is no tomorrow or yesterday

where it ends and begins

cause for this life

we must let go

and hope for a place

greater than this one

—i will wait for you at heaven's gate

a flicker of light may seem more beautiful

but a spark of fire that never yields

lasts forever

your love for me touched

every corner of this world

wrapped in rhymes and phrases

my love for you will stay here

hidden in my heart

never to be given away

to someone

who will never love you

like i did

would you still love me if I were not blonde?

she asked

that made me question

all the *what-ifs* between us

as I looked at the screen

I asked her in my mind

would you still love me if I was disloyal?

would you still look for me if I keep on hiding?

would you still make me your muse if I lost myself?

would you still come back if you can't remember me?

would you still chase me if I was no longer fun?

what about if I need you more than you need me?

—all the questions I don't want you to answer

BLACK SNOWMAN

the rest of the world died

when your eyes met mine

no so perfect me

perfectly in love

with your light

and for the first time

this darkness in me

craved the light

BLACK SNOWMAN

you loved him because *he loves you*

you loved me because *you love me*

but he was the *ocean* and I a *river*

nobody notices *a pebble*,

when they are looking for *the mountain*

I felt so small

as the *breeze* battled the *storm*

I offered you my forever that night

because I could not simply

stand in the corner

and watch you fall in love

with *someone* who is *not me*

—*i am sorry, i lost the war*

promises are not as beautiful as they sound

but if one day

someone tells me

an old woman with blonde hair

waits for me by the front gate

there will not be a single soul

in this world

who could stop me

from bringing her home

when I stood up for a girl

against a hundred men that night

I knew you'd stand

against a thousand men

and torture a million souls

just for staring at me

—i miss you

some people are not worth our time

but some people deserve to hold us

in every lifetime

still, this fractured soul within

will never reach for her *halo*

and the shadow that dwells inside

can never claim her *sun*

my silence fractured your time

freeze your undying soul

but couldn't hold your dying memories of me

and every day when i wake up

it gets harder to breathe

to be loved and forgotten

i am silenced by your pain

guess i'll stay a stranger

in your head once again

but i have no complaint

i own your sweet soul

i'm good

BLACK SNOWMAN

she smiles beneath a sky

that belongs to another

his shadow towers like mountains

a single pebble waits

at the foot of impossibility

love whispers, unheard

and destiny keeps its silence

fantasies of realities

remembered by no one

are haunting me

there's no you except in my sleep

tell me, was it even real?

should I sleep forever to be by your side?

or freeze into a memory

from a past *that is no longer mine*

BLACK SNOWMAN

mountains rise

where hearts cannot climb

and rivers carry words that fade before reaching

i wait quietly at the valley's edge

knowing she will never come down

the only soul i want

to be my right one

not to be possessed

not to be forgotten either

and the heart keeps her seat

though she walks another path

some things are not ours

and they should never be ours

because *love* goes both ways

so does *respect*

and so does *honesty*

My entire life I have listened to thousands of sad lullabies, I could send you songs you will play on repeat for years, but all these songs cannot bring you back to me, *right?*

BLACK SNOWMAN

there is a scripture

you left behind

that says

i write you so much

my pen wonders if you are my god

and i laughed bitter

for what kind of god

meets his worshipper in shadows

kisses her where borders burn

and hides his devotion

like contraband beneath the soil

yet your words haunt me

a girl writing me into divinity

while i remain a boy

damned by blood and tongue

searching your scripture

for forgiveness

neither of us will ever receive

I fear I have no choice

but to believe you

when you said

you were going to come and find me

—wherever you are in this chaotic world

fighting against giants and monsters

to return home to me

I hope you arrive safely in my arms

I AM WAITING.

BLACK SNOWMAN

ACKNOWLEDGMENTS

Thank you to my muse, Black Snowman, for allowing me to write your story—now you will never be forgotten.

To Mom, Nard & Sophie —my family

To Florence, for the line; *"you love him because he loves you"*

To my amazing chosen family, *Dragons & Chickens—you've changed me forever!*

To *Felkima*, for being my constant listener in this journey called *Life.*

To my beloved juniors, *Alona & Dari—thank you for the warm food and genuine words.*

To Blu—*you are stuck with me for life.*

And last, but definitely not least~

To *Mapuia*, for choosing me in this life

—you are the lemon of my life.

ABOUT THE AUTHOR

Olivia Remsangpuii (born April 7, 2003) is an Indian-Mizo poet and author.

She published her debut English poetry book, *"Neverland,"* at the age of 18.

After three long years of break in her writing, she published her second poetry book *"Black Snowman"* at the age of 21.

—the very book you are holding in your hands.

She has made significant contributions to the realm of literature, including articles, poetry, essays, and songs.

In 2019, she introduced the acrostic writing style to the National Competition, and her writings were featured in periodicals across North-East India.

The work of Olivia Remsangpuii evolves from time to time with phases of her life and the people she met along the way.

In the process of writing *Black Snowman,* the author reflected her love for the character during an icy winter in 2023, which prompted her return to the realm of poetry.

Olivia is a writer who transforms real-life experiences into works that blur the line between memory and art. Her writing is marked by honesty, intensity, and a timeless search for meaning.

At present, she has withdrawn from the outside world, finding solitude in her room, where she studies the stars, delves into astrology, and continues her journey of healing from illness.

A MESSAGE FROM THE AUTHOR

This life is full of broken promises, unnoticed signboards, forgotten lovers, and forgiven liars. I live my days wondering why life cannot be as glorious as we read in poetry—*I will never figure out why.*

But don't you think it is amazing to forget everything for a brief moment—the rules, the hatred, the worries of tomorrow—*and just follow your stupid little heart?*

This life is too short to let go of the person you love the most

—*I hope you have the courage to chase the butterfly before you.*

But if one day this life offers a fresh apple and a lemon before you—*I hope you have the courage to choose the lemon.*

This life is already too hard and confusing; we cannot choose the family we came from, but we have all the authority to choose the family coming from us—*I hope you choose wisely.*

Thank you for reading Black Snowman!

With Guilt

The Author

BLACK SNOWMAN

BLACK SNOWMAN

and for this lifetime

i lost you, snow